THE ESSENTIAL
HARRY STYLES
FANBOOK

MORTIMER

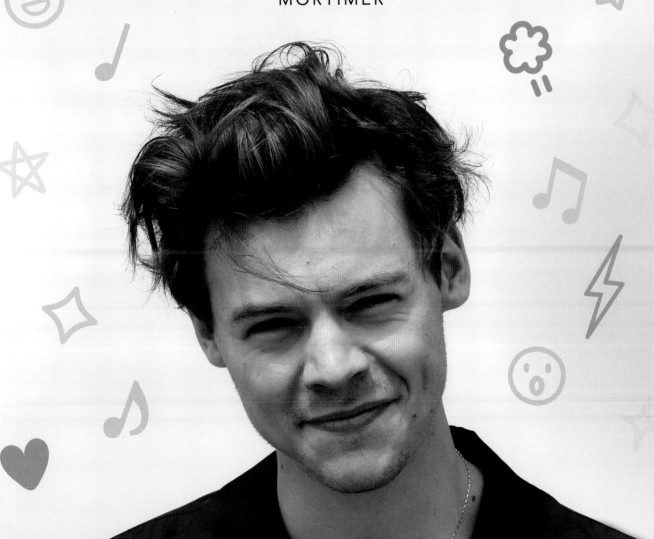

Published in 2023 by Mortimer Children's
An Imprint of Welbeck Children's Limited,
part of the Welbeck Publishing Group

Offices in:
London - 20 Mortimer Street, London W1T 3JW &
Sydney - Level 17, 207 Kent St, Sydney NSW 2000 Australia

www.welbeckpublishing.com

Text and design © Welbeck Children's Limited 2023

The publishers would like to thank the following sources for their kind permission to reproduce the pictures in this book.

ALAMY: Retro AdArchives 28L; TCD/Prod.DB 24R; Vertigo Entertainment/Album 24BL

GETTY IMAGES: Axelle/Bauer-Griffin/FilmMagic 9BR; Scott Barbour 10L, 51; Bauer-Griffin/GC Images 27BR; David M. Benett 6BL, 46C; Bettmann 21TL; Gustavo Caballero 46BL; Gilbert Carrasquillo/GC Images 31TR; Gareth Cattermole 46R; Dominique Charriau/WireImage 27BL; Mark Davis 46BR; James Devaney/GC Images 12-13; Dia Dipasupil 26, 31TL; Scott Dudelson/Wireimage 44-45; Shirlaine Forrest/WireImage 8R, 46L; Rich Fury 30B, 57; Gary Gershoff 60; Taylor Hill/FilmMagic 55BR; Dave J Hogan 9C, 34-35, 47BC; Arturo Holmes 34L; Samir Hussein/WireImage 59; JMEnternational 28R; JNI/Star Max/GC Images 61; Dimitrios Kambouris 56; Jeff Kravitz/FilmMagic 55TL; J. Lee/FilmMagic 47L; Francois Lo Presti/AFP 1C, 10TR; Kevin Mazur 2-3, 6L, 7, 10BR, 21R, 21BR, 22-23, 27BCL, 30TR, 32-33, 36-37, 42-43, 47TR, 49, 52-53, 54; Jamie McCarthy/GC Images 47TC; MEGA/GC Images 47BR; Neil Mockford/FilmMagic 8BL; Neil Mockford/GC Images 25L, 27TL; James D. Morgan/WireImage 16-17; Steve Morley/Redferns 20R; Joseph Okpako/Wireimage 40-41; Cindy Ord 14; Anthony Pham 4-5, 29; Brian Rasic/Wireimage 39TL; Alexi Rosenfeld 11R; Monica Schipper 36R; John Shearer 37BL; Rocco Spaziani/Archivio Spaziani/Mondadori Portfolio 25B; Amy Sussman 31BL; Karwai Tang 30TL, 39B, 47C; Lorne Thomson/Redferns 38BL; Jack Vartoogian 20L; Elisabetta A. Villa 18-19, 30TC; Theo Wargo 27BCR, 37TL; Matt Winkelmeyer 11BL; Kevin Winter 31BR, 38R, 62-63

SHUTTERSTOCK: Doomu 9L; Ihor Hvozdetskyi 8L; Jeonghyeon Noh 11TL; Mrs.Siwaporn 11TR; Olexandr Taranukhin 34-35BKG

ISBN 978 1 83935 252 2

Printed in Heshan, China

10 9 8 7 6 5 4 3 2 1

★ CONTENTS

WELCOME

ARE YOU A TOTAL HARRY OBSESSIVE AND A FULL-FLEDGED STYLERS MEMBER?

THEN THIS IS THE BOOK FOR YOU—PACKED WITH FUN FACTS, MUST-SEE PICS AND SONGWRITING TIPS, PLUS LOTS MORE ABOUT THE WORLD'S FAVORITE SINGER, SONGWRITER, ACTOR, AND FASHION ICON.

WHAT'S MORE, YOU CAN FIND OUT WHICH CHART-TOPPING TRACKS HARRY WROTE FOR OTHER ARTISTS AND TEST YOUR FAN KNOWLEDGE WITH OUR BIG QUIZ.

★ MEET HARRY

THIS IS YOUR CHANCE TO HANG OUT WITH THE REAL HARRY—THE GUY BEHIND SOME OF THE MOST-STREAMED SONGS IN HISTORY WHO'S NOW TAKING THE FASHION AND MOVIE INDUSTRY BY STORM.

THE STYLES FILES:

NAME:	Harry Edward Styles
FROM:	Worcestershire, England
DATE OF BIRTH:	February 1, 1994
EDUCATION:	Holmes Chapel Comprehensive School, Cheshire, England
FIRST BAND:	White Eskimo (while at school)
STAR SIGN:	Aquarius
EYE COLOR:	Green
SPECIAL SKILL:	Juggling
MOM:	Anne Twist
DAD:	Desmond Styles
STEPDAD:	Robin Twist
SIBLINGS:	Gemma (big sister)
STEPSIBLINGS:	Mike & Amy

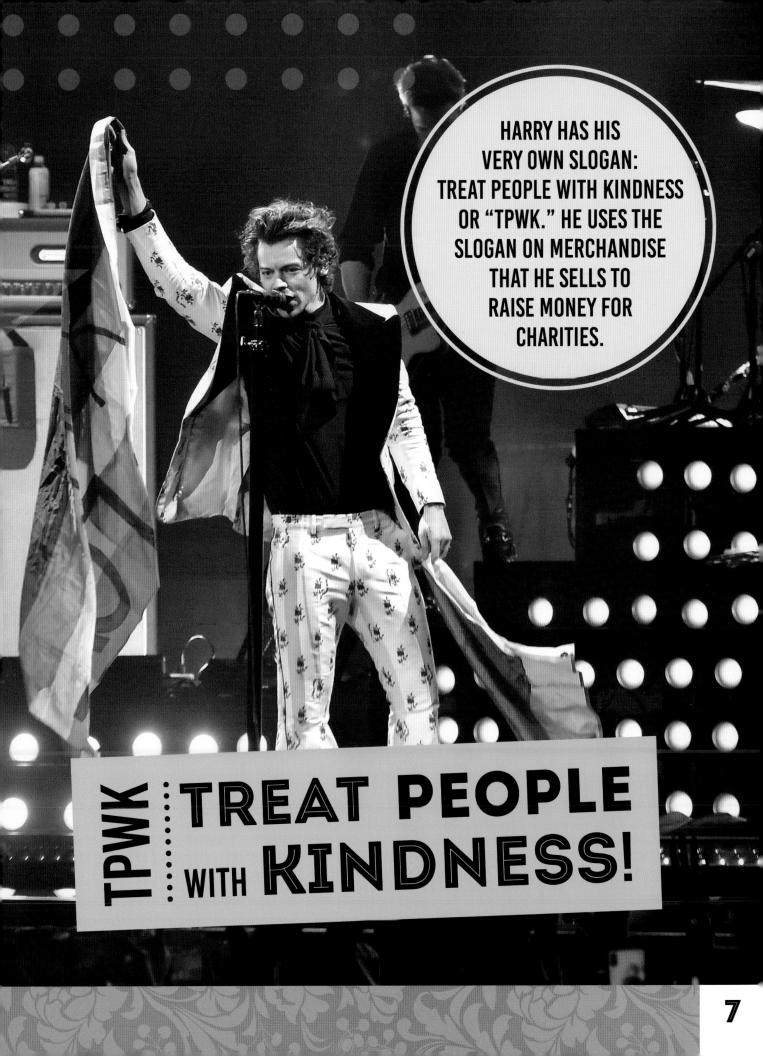

HARRY HAS HIS VERY OWN SLOGAN: TREAT PEOPLE WITH KINDNESS OR "TPWK." HE USES THE SLOGAN ON MERCHANDISE THAT HE SELLS TO RAISE MONEY FOR CHARITIES.

TPWK : TREAT **PEOPLE** WITH **KINDNESS!**

HOW IT STARTED VS. HOW IT'S GOING

SINCE BURSTING ONTO THE MUSIC SCENE IN 2011 AS A MEMBER OF ONE DIRECTION, HARRY HAS GONE ONTO DOMINATE THE POP WORLD... AND PRETTY MUCH EVERYTHING ELSE FOR THAT MATTER!

SATURDAY JOB

When Harry was a teenager, he earned money by working at a local bakery. His boss from back then described young Harry as the most polite member of staff they ever had.

TASTE OF STARDOM

Harry's first taste of the popstar life was being in a band called White Eskimo. The pop-punk band performed at a wedding and lots of talent shows.

X FACTOR

But it was of course his *X Factor* audition that changed Harry's life. He was just 16 years old when he sang *Isn't She Lovely* by Stevie Wonder in front of Simon Cowell, Nicole Scherzinger, and Louis Walsh.

1D

Further along in the audition process, Harry was put into a five-piece band along with Liam Payne, Niall Horan, Louis Tomlinson, and Zayn Malik. The soloists were put together by Simon Cowell to form a band who we now know as One Direction.

DEBUT HIT

1D (One Direction) came third in *The X Factor* and went on to have five UK number-one singles, including their first release, *What Makes You Beautiful*. Their debut album *Up All Night* even made pop history as the first band to debut with a number-one album in the US.

THE BREAK

In 2016, the much-loved and phenomenally successful 1D took a break for the band members to pursue their own solo projects. While fans were heartbroken at the time, this was when Harry really found his feet in the music industry.

SOLO SIGN-UP

He signed with Columbia Records (the same label as 1D) as a solo artist in the same year and by 2017 Harry released his debut single *Sign of the Times*. It was such a hit that it smashed Ed Sheeran's *Shape of You* single off the top spot after 13 weeks at number one.

MAKING A MOVIE

At the same time as going solo, Harry was also filming his first movie set in World War II called *Dunkirk*.

SECOND ALBUM

Fine Line was released in 2019, and it included hits such as *Watermelon Sugar* and *Treat People with Kindness*. Debuting at number one on the Billboard 200, *Fine Line* was Harry's second number-one album in the US.

SOLO SUCCESS

His highly anticipated album, *Harry Styles*, came out in 2017 too, and it reached number one in heaps of countries around the world. But Harry didn't stop there. He then went on his first tour.

VOGUE COVER

In 2020, Harry became Vogue's first ever solo male cover star. He wore a gown and tuxedo, and this boundary-pushing got lots of people talking about masculinity and gender.

VIRAL VIDEOS

The premiere of the music video for *Watermelon Sugar* in 2020 is one of the star's biggest successes. It racked up 8 million views in only 15 hours! Fans could not get enough of the video, which features Harry on a Malibu beach wearing a crochet vest and oversized blue sunnies. He also received a Grammy and a Brit Award for this track

SILVER SCREEN

Following the positive response to Harry's acting debut in *Dunkirk*, he was in two more big movies in 2022—*Don't Worry Darling* and *My Policeman*.

THIRD ALBUM

Just when you thought Harry Styles mania couldn't get any bigger, he released his third album, *Harry's House*. It was the fastest-selling album in the UK for 2022. Four singles from the album made it into the top 10 at the same time—only The Beatles managed this before, and that was in 1964.

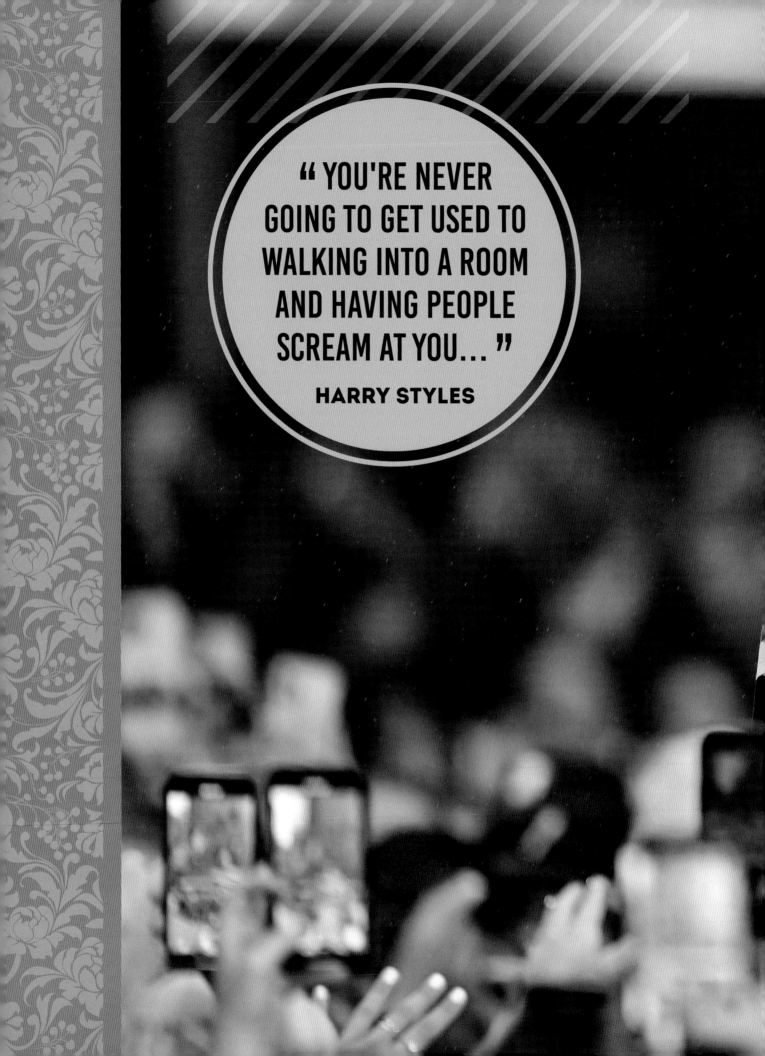

" YOU'RE NEVER GOING TO GET USED TO WALKING INTO A ROOM AND HAVING PEOPLE SCREAM AT YOU… "

HARRY STYLES

HARRY
BY NUMBERS

12 YEARS
since Harry auditioned
FOR THE X FACTOR
and was placed in
ONE DIRECTION

1994 BORN
IN WORCESTERSHIRE,
ENGLAND

AS IT WAS
15 weeks at
Billboard
HOT 100

HARRY WAS ONLY 16 YEARS OLD WHEN HE FIRST ROSE TO FAME

RANKED 491 IN THE 2020 Rolling Stone GREATEST ALBUMS OF ALL TIME with his album, FINE LINE

MORE THAN 47.9M Instagram followers

221 WEEKS IN UK'S TOP 75 SINGLES CHART

2 US NUMBER 1s

NOW ABOVE 1.5 BILLION STREAMS ON SPOTIFY for HARRY'S HOUSE

IN 2017 HE made his feature FILM DEBUT IN DUNKIRK

ONE DIRECTION SOLD 70 MILLION RECORDS

2021 OPENED THE GRAMMY AWARDS with WATERMELON SUGAR

CHART-TOPPING HITS

WHEN IT COMES TO SMASHING THE CHARTS, THERE'S NO DENYING THAT HARRY IS THE KING. HE'S NOTCHED A BUNCH OF BIG HITS, BUT HERE ARE THE GREATEST OF ALL FROM THE MIX...

SIGN OF THE TIMES

This breakout anthem was Harry's first solo single after One Direction. It reached number four in the US charts.

Released: 2017

LIGHTS UP

This synth-pop track was a bit of a departure from Harry's signature rocky-poppy vibe, and it went over sensationally well. It racked up 76 million UK chart sales and reached number three in the charts.

Released: 2019

WATERMELON SUGAR

Not only did the music video go viral, but the song became the second-longest-running chart song of all time in the UK. It's all about the excitement of a new romance.

Released: 2019

> **" IF YOU'RE HAPPY DOING WHAT YOU LOVE, NOBODY CAN TELL YOU YOU'RE NOT SUCCESSFUL. "**
>
> **HARRY STYLES**

ADORE YOU

This upbeat love song peaked at number seven and it's just too catchy not to sing along whenever you hear it.

Released: 2019

LATE NIGHT TALKING

As the second single from *Harry's House*, this track peaked at number three in the charts. But *Late Night Talking* was actually the number-one trending song in the UK.

Released: 2022

AS IT WAS

This is another of his songs we never seem to get sick of, and it became the longest-running number one in the US by a UK act. It also reached number one in the UK, too!

Released: 2022

10 REASONS WE LOVE HARRY

IT WAS A CHALLENGE TO WHITTLE THIS DOWN TO JUST 10 REASONS, BUT HERE YOU GO...

1 He always makes the EFFORT to INTERACT with his fans.

2 HE'S HUMBLE. He doesn't take his fame and success for granted, which isn't easy when you've been in the spotlight from such a young age.

3 ADVENTUROUS STYLE! Harry is not afraid to break the mold by wearing flamboyant clothes from dresses to frilly collars to feather boas and pearls!

4 HE'S PASSIONATE. In 2022 Harry inspired 54,000 new voters to register for elections in America, by offering fans the chance to attend his Harryween costume party.

5 HE WRITES SONGS... and lots of them. He doesn't just write for himself either but for plenty of big artists!

6 HE SPEAKS OUT about important issues, from gender equality and supporting the LGBTQ+ community to Black Lives Matter.

7 HE'S KIND. So kind, that he has his own kindness mantra, Treat People with Kindness, or TPWK.

8 HARRY IS AUTHENTIC. He's stayed true to himself and doesn't change to fit in with anyone.

9 When Harry donated his luscious locks to the Little Princess Trust, he proved just how CARING he is.

10 He's all about making people feel accepted. His community is non-judgemental and a place for fans to FEEL SAFE AND WELCOME.

19

★ HARRY'S IDOLS

THE PHENOMENON OF HARRY STYLES CONTINUES TO BRING PEOPLE TOGETHER, REGARDLESS OF AGE OR GENDER—NO WONDER HE'S BEEN COMPARED TO MUSIC LEGEND DAVID BOWIE. SO WHERE DOES THIS SUPERSTAR TAKE HIS INSPIRATION FROM?

DAVID BOWIE

It takes guts to put your own songs out into the world, and it turns out even megastars like Harry can feel the pressure. But Harry was inspired by David Bowie's comforting words in an interview where he said it's ok to feel uncomfortable about a song.

PAUL SIMON

If there was a soundtrack to his youth, Harry says it would be Paul Simon. He's a massive fan and thinks some of his melodies are the best ever written.

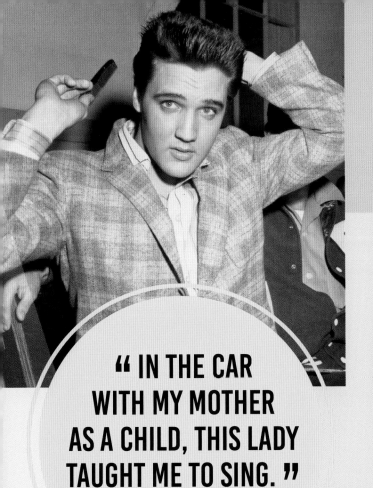

ELVIS PRESLEY

The first music that Harry ever heard was the King of Rock and Roll himself, Elvis Presley. He used to sing Elvis songs on his karaoke machine, and his grandfather would film him. So cute!

" IN THE CAR WITH MY MOTHER AS A CHILD, THIS LADY TAUGHT ME TO SING. "

HARRY STYLES
ON SHANIA TWAIN

SHANIA TWAIN

The country singer behind 90s hits such as *Man! I Feel Like A Woman* was a big part of Harry's life growing up.

CAROLE KING

Another influence is the iconic American singer-songwriter Carole King, who wrote her first number-one hit aged just 17 with *Will You Love Me Tomorrow*. Harry's favorite track is *So Far Away*.

FLEETWOOD MAC

Harry often says that Fleetwood Mac has inspired his own sound. He once did a cover of their song *The Chain* for the BBC back in 2017.

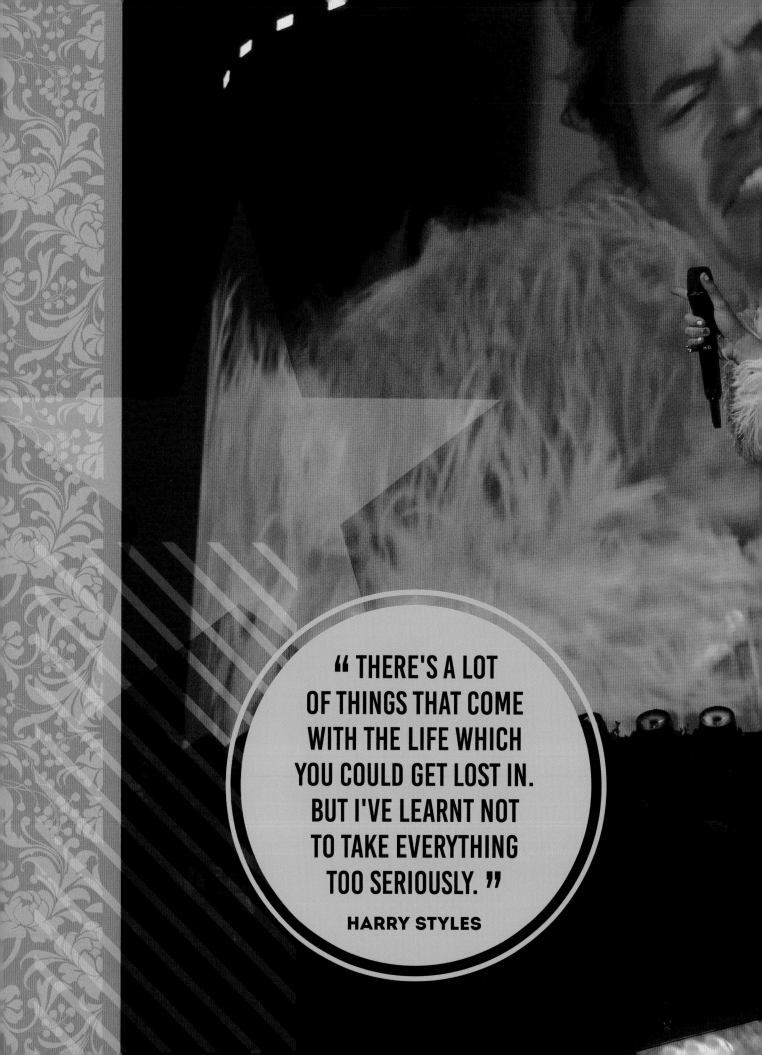

" THERE'S A LOT OF THINGS THAT COME WITH THE LIFE WHICH YOU COULD GET LOST IN. BUT I'VE LEARNT NOT TO TAKE EVERYTHING TOO SERIOUSLY. "

HARRY STYLES

STAR OF THE SILVER SCREEN

AS IF SINGING AND SONGWRITING WASN'T ENOUGH, HARRY NOW ALSO HAS A MOVIE CAREER TO BOOT. IS THERE NO END TO THIS GUY'S TALENTS? CHECK OUT HIS MOVIE APPEARANCES SO FAR…

DUNKIRK, 2017

Playing a soldier called Alex, Harry made his acting debut in *Dunkirk*—a powerful movie about the Battle of Dunkirk during World War II. It was during this movie that The experience of filming really sparked Harry's love of acting, and we're hardly surprised—he was working alongside the likes of Tom Hardy and Kenneth Branagh, after all!

DON'T WORRY DARLING, 2022

Having proven himself as a credible actor, *Don't Worry Darling* is Harry's first major role in a movie. He stars alongside the powerhouse that is Florence Pugh (Alice) as her husband Jack in this period drama come thriller, which is set in the 1950s.

MY POLICEMAN, 2022

An adaption of Bethan Roberts' novel *My Policeman*, this romantic movie is about a love-triangle involving a teacher, a policeman, and a curator. Harry plays the police constable called Tom in this story about forbidden love.

ETERNALS, 2021
CAMEO APPEARANCE

Harry debuted in the Marvel Cinematic Universe (MCU) with a super brief appearance in *Eternals* where he played Eros, brother of Thanos and also known as Starfox. His onscreen partner for this iconic moment was Pip, a CGI character. Rumor has it that Harry will be returning to the Marvel Cinematic Universe. Cross your fingers!

" IT'S FUN TO PLAY IN WORLDS THAT AREN'T NECESSARILY YOUR OWN. "

HARRY STYLES

QUIZ — WHAT'S YOUR HARRY STYLE?

TRY OUT THIS FUN QUIZ TO DISCOVER WHICH OF HARRY'S LOOKS SUMS YOU UP! PICK **A, B, C,** OR **D** FOR EACH QUESTION, AND DON'T FORGET TO KEEP NOTE OF YOUR ANSWERS.

1 What word would your bestie use to describe you?
- **A.** Leader
- **B.** Loud
- **C.** Funny
- **D.** Cool

2 Choose your dream vacation destination.
- **A.** Luxury ski lodge
- **B.** Music festival
- **C.** Sight-seeing city break
- **D.** Chilling out on a beach

3 What's your favorite celebration?
- **A.** Valentine's Day
- **B.** New Year's Eve
- **C.** Halloween
- **D.** Birthday

4 Pick a hobby you'd like to try.
- **A.** Skiing
- **B.** Rock climbing
- **C.** Dancing
- **D.** Surfing

5 Pick your favorite drink.
- **A.** Hot choc with all the trimmings
- **B.** Lemonade
- **C.** Milkshake
- **D.** Water

6 How would you spend your perfect Saturday?

A. Pamper day

B. Bowling

C. Shopping

D. Playing videogames

7 What would be your dream job?

A. Model

B. Singer

C. Comedian

D. Artist

8 How much do you enjoy being center of attention?

A. Love it!

B. It's mostly okay.

C. Hmm, I don't mind it...

D. Hate it!

MOSTLY **A**s =
Luxe Harry

You have a taste for the finer things in life, so your Harry Style is luxe. You are all about indulgence and love an excuse to pamper yourself and dress up, so bring on the velvet and the bling!

MOSTLY **B**s =
Party Harry

You are here for the party look, so don your spangly jumpsuit and fling as many sequins at yourself as you can. The more color, glitter, and fun the better!

MOSTLY **C**s =
Harryween Harry

Your closet's filled with costumes, and you don't need any excuse to dress up. There's nothing more fun than a themed party, which is why Halloween is your favorite season.

MOSTLY **D**s =
Cool Harry

You are the master of the chilled-out vibe. You're most comfortable in your beanie and t-shirt, and you make it look so good!

HARRY THE FASHION ICON

FROM HIS GUCCI COLLECTION TO BEING THE FIRST SOLO MAN TO MAKE IT ONTO THE COVER OF VOGUE, HARRY SURE KNOWS HOW TO TURN HEADS FOR ALL THE RIGHT REASONS.

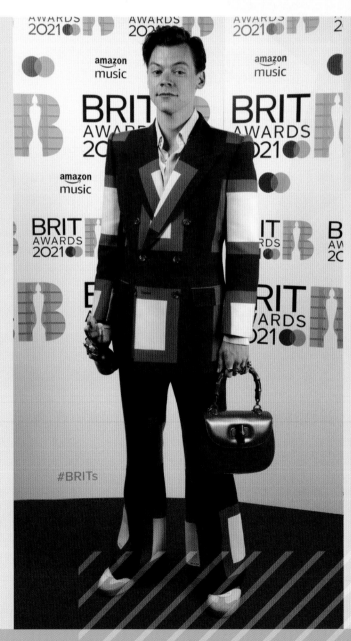

GUCCI HA HA HA

The fashion house describes their Harry Styles collection as playful. Like most things Harry touches, the looks are quirky, bold, and full of personality. Why is it called HA HA HA? It's the way that friends Harry and Alessandro Michele (Creative Director of Gucci) have always signed off their text messages to each other. Yep, the pair are good buds!

PLEASING

Not content with singing, songwriting, and acting, Harry also launched his very own beauty brand called Pleasing. There are lots of celebrities with makeup and beauty brands out there, but unsurprisingly, Harry's stands out. Created for men and women, Harry's collection includes bold shades that can be applied to lips, eyes, or body, plus bright nail polishes.

EVEN AS FAR BACK AS HIS 1D DAYS, HARRY'S NEVER BEEN AFRAID TO EXPERIMENT WITH FASHION. HIS BOLD FASHION CHOICES HAVE CAUGHT THE ATTENTION OF FASHIONISTAS EVERYWHERE!

VOGUE COVER

For his history-making Vogue cover shoot, Harry wore a lacy white dress with a black tuxedo jacket. The issue flew off the shelves so quickly, they had to rush to print more! We love how Harry is challenging traditional men's fashion.

HARRY'S STYLES

LET'S CELEBRATE SOME OF OUR MOST FAVORITE AND BOLD LOOKS!

Talk about a statement collar!

A sheer black blouse with a single pearl earring makes for an iconic Met Gala look.

Only Harry could make a polka-dot sweater vest look edgy!

Here's a loud suit that would make Austin Powers green with envy!

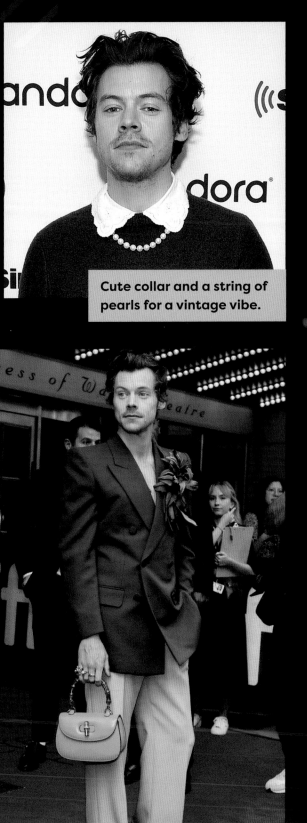

Cute collar and a string of pearls for a vintage vibe.

It's all about the accessories.

What's not to love about those bold diagonal stripes with flared sleeves?

Double leather for the win!

HARRY'S AWARDS

THE KING OF POP IS RACKING UP A SERIOUSLY IMPRESSIVE COLLECTION OF AWARDS—LET'S HOPE HE HAS A DISPLAY CABINET BIG ENOUGH TO HOUSE THEM ALL. HERE ARE SOME OF THE ONES HE'S WON!

2022

MTV VIDEO MUSIC AWARDS
- Best Cinematography for *As It Was*
- Best Pop for *As It Was*
- Album of the Year for *Harry's House*

GRAMMY AWARDS
2021
Best Pop Solo Performance for *Watermelon Sugar*

JUNO AWARDS
2021
International Album of the Year for *Fine Line*

MTV MIAW
Global Hit of the Year for *Golden*
2021

MTV VIDEO MUSIC AWARDS

2021

Best Choreography for *Treat People with Kindness*

iHEARTRADIO MUSIC AWARDS

2021

Best Lyrics for *Adore You*

iHEARTRADIO MUSIC AWARDS

2019

Best Cover Song for *You're Still the One* (shared with Kacey Musgraves)

iHEARTRADIO MUSIC AWARDS

2018

- Best Cover Song for *The Chain*
- Best Music Video for *Sign of the Times*

TEEN CHOICE AWARDS

2014

Choice Smile

TEEN CHOICE AWARDS

2013

Choice Smile
Choice Male Hottie

★ COOL COLLABS

ONE SUREFIRE WAY TO SPOT A TRUE MUSICAL LEGEND IS BY LOOKING AT THE ARTISTS THEY'VE COLLABORATED WITH. IT'S HARDLY SURPRISING THEN THAT HARRY HAS WRITTEN FOR AND PERFORMED WITH SOME OF THE BIGGEST LEGENDS AROUND. HERE ARE SOME FAVORITES...

JOHN LEGEND

Back in 2014, Harry teamed up with John Legend and co-wrote a track. This was his first project away from One Direction—what a way to kick off a solo career!

LIZZO

During Coachella 2022, Harry joined Lizzo on stage to perform One Direction's *What Makes You Beautiful*, and Gloria Gaynor's *I Will Survive*. Needless to say, the fans went wild for the duo!

STORMZY

The iconic British rapper, Stormzy, was a surprise guest at Harry's intimate London gig in 2019. Together they sang Stormzy's *Vossi Bop*.

STEVIE NICKS

This duo's friendship blossomed after meeting at a Fleetwood Mac concert in 2015. Since then, they have taken turns joining each other on stage to perform together.

KACEY MUSGRAVES

Country met pop when singer Kacey supported Harry on his 2018 tour. That same year she and Harry took to the stage for a one-off duet of Shania Twain's epic single, *You're Still The One*.

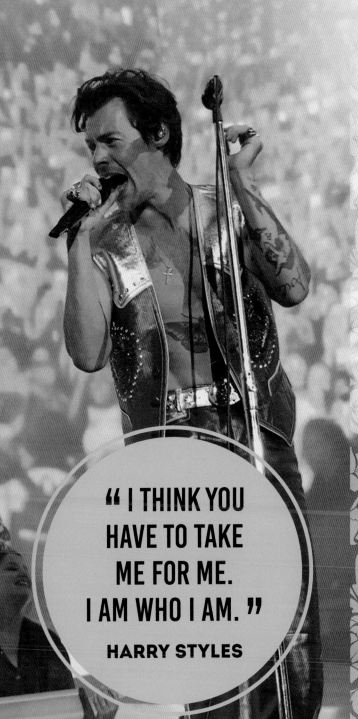

" I THINK YOU HAVE TO TAKE ME FOR ME. I AM WHO I AM. "

HARRY STYLES

WRITING FOR THE STARS

BESIDES WRITING WRITING HEAPS OF HIS OWN MUSIC, HARRY HAS ALSO SHARED THE LOVE BY CREATING BIG HITS FOR OTHER ARTISTS.

ARIANA GRANDE'S *JUST A LITTLE BIT OF YOUR HEART*

Harry co-wrote Ariana's 2014 hit *Just a Little Bit of Your Heart* with Johan Carlsson. The emotional track features on Ariana's second album *My Everything*. Harry has actually performed the track while touring—so not all his fans will be surprised to hear this! Let's cross everything that this duo sing together some day...

BLEACHERS' *ALFIE'S SONG* (*NOT SO TYPICAL LOVE SONG*)

The song was co-written by Harry Styles along with Jack Antonoff and Ilsey Juber. The song features on the movie soundtrack to *Love, Simon*.

MICHAEL BUBLÉ'S *SOMEDAY*

Are you a Bublé fan? Well, you may have heard his track featuring vocals by Meghan Trainor. It's called *Someday* and it's on his ninth album, *Nobody But Me*. What might surprise you is that this song was co-written by none other than Meghan Trainor and Harry Styles.

ONE DIRECTION DAYS

Did you know that Harry co-wrote some of One Direction's biggest songs? He contributed to three tracks on their debut album *Up All Night*—*Taken*, *Everything About You* and *Same Mistakes*. He continued to co-write tracks across their albums, including their number-one hit, *Story of My Life*.

HARRY'S TOP 5 MUSIC VIDEOS

WHEN IT COMES TO HARRY STYLES' MUSIC VIDEOS, THERE'S PLENTY TO LOVE ABOUT ALL OF THEM. BUT HERE ARE FIVE OF HIS TOP VIDS AND WHY THEY'RE JUST SO GREAT.

BEST MOVES

▶ AS IT WAS

If you're a fan of Harry's dance moves, then check out this video. He starts off wearing a bright red coat, which comes off to reveal a red spangled jumpsuit as he busts out the moves. Iconic. The lyrics and the video are full of emotion and are made that extra bit beautiful with his expressive dancing on a turntable.

▶ MUSIC FOR A SUSHI RESTAURANT

This one is probably one of Harry's most unusual music videos to date. It involves him wriggling around as human-squid hybrid on the floor of (you guessed it!) a sushi restaurant. Harry wrote the song and said he was inspired while eating in a sushi restaurant. The song is just super catchy, and the video is mesmerizing!

MOST ORIGINAL

MOST VIEWED

▶ SIGN OF THE TIMES

Harry's dramatic debut single as a soloist has racked up an immense 1 billion views on YouTube. It's a powerful song with an equally powerful video—think Harry taking off and gliding over a stormy coastline with uber moody weather and crashing seas.

BEST FOR ESCAPISM

▶ *GOLDEN*

This hopeful and uplifting track is all about sunshine, picturesque Italian scenery, and arty shots! What's not to love about this chilled-out tune from Harry? He said he wanted to bring joy with this number and imagined people listening to it as they drive along the coast (like he does in the video!).

ALL THE NOSTAGLIA

▶ *TREAT PEOPLE WITH KINDNESS*

The fun black-and-white video sees Harry and the one and only Phoebe Waller-Bridge dancing around as a double act in this 1920s-inspired dance routine. Word has it that Harry asked Phoebe to be in his video after watching her perform on stage. What a double act!

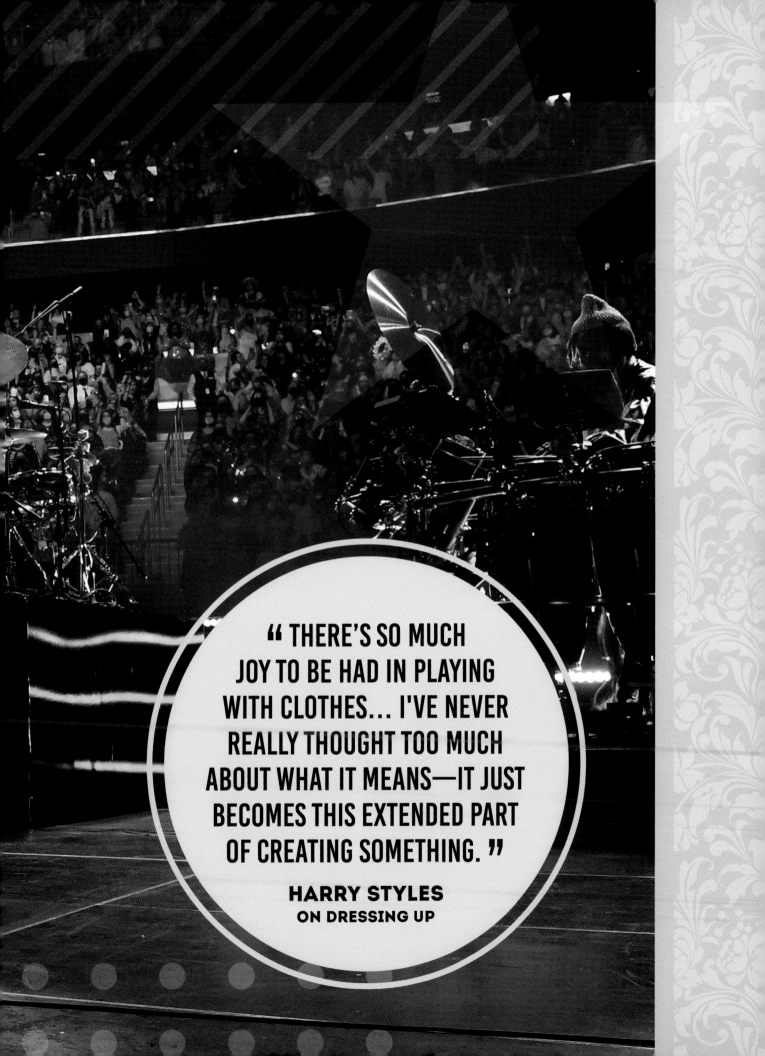

" THERE'S SO MUCH JOY TO BE HAD IN PLAYING WITH CLOTHES... I'VE NEVER REALLY THOUGHT TOO MUCH ABOUT WHAT IT MEANS—IT JUST BECOMES THIS EXTENDED PART OF CREATING SOMETHING. "

HARRY STYLES
ON DRESSING UP

11 THINGS YOU DIDN'T KNOW ABOUT HARRY

SO YOU CALL YOURSELF A HARRY STYLES SUPERFAN? SEE HOW MANY OF THESE ARE NEWS TO YOU.

1 Harry is a mad about Shania! He claims that Shania Twain is not only a huge influence in his music but also on his fashion.

2 He appeared in an episode of the Nickelodeon show *iCarly* alongside his 1D bandmates. The episode was called *iGo One Direction*.

3 Harry has more than 40 tattoos. They range from a large butterfly on his torso (probably one of his best-known tattoos!) to a pair of swallows and initials of family members.

4 In his first school play, Harry played the role of a church mouse called Barney. Harry said he loved dressing up as the character.

5 He loves romantic comedies and is especially fond of *The Notebook*.

6 Fleetwood Mac's Stevie Nicks wants to adopt Harry. She says he's "the son I never had."

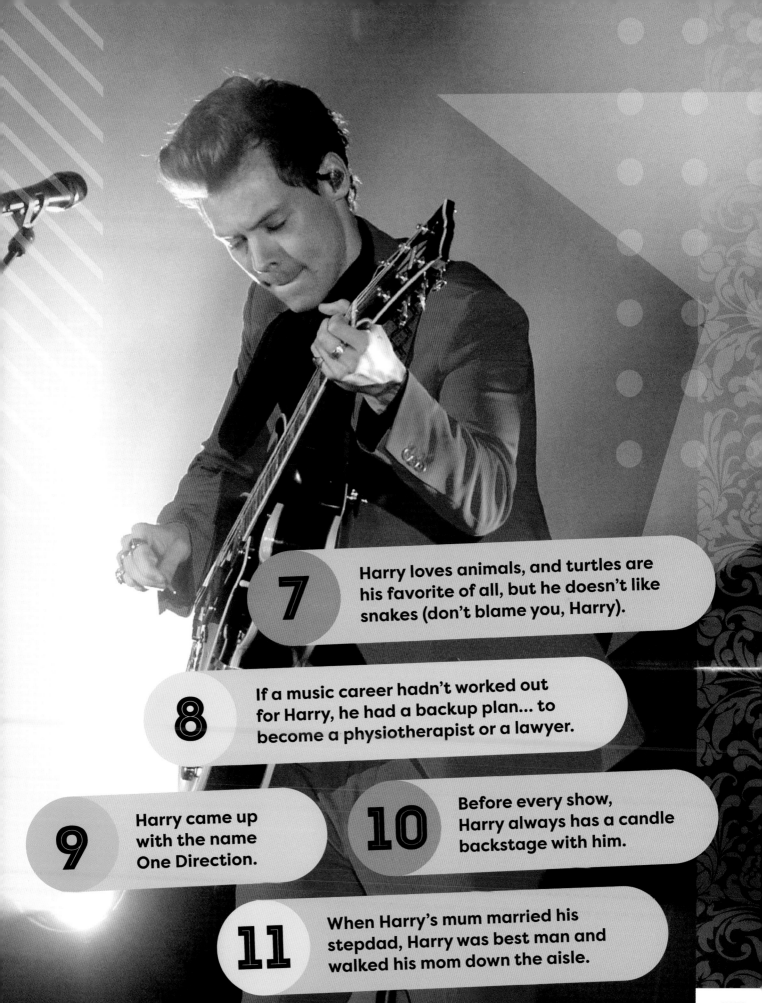

7 Harry loves animals, and turtles are his favorite of all, but he doesn't like snakes (don't blame you, Harry).

8 If a music career hadn't worked out for Harry, he had a backup plan... to become a physiotherapist or a lawyer.

9 Harry came up with the name One Direction.

10 Before every show, Harry always has a candle backstage with him.

11 When Harry's mum married his stepdad, Harry was best man and walked his mom down the aisle.

HAIRY STYLES

WITH THOSE THICK AND UBER-GLOSSY WAVES, IT SEEMS HARRY CAN DO NO WRONG WHEN IT COMES TO EXPERIMENTING WITH HAIRSTYLES. WHETHER IT'S LONG OR SHORT, SIDE-SWEPT, OR COIFFED, HARRY'S MANE ALWAYS EXCELS. LET'S CELEBRATE SOME OF HIS ICONIC LOOKS.

Big bouncy curls from way back in the early 1D days.

Who didn't adore this uber stylish side sweep?!

We all remember when Harry stepped out with this slick swept-back coif.

Long hair don't care!

And that's how you stand out in a boy band!

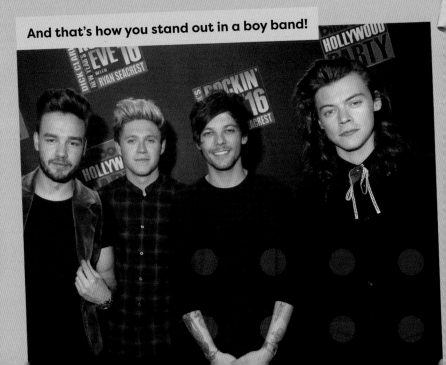

This quiff could rival Elvis Presley's.

Festival vibes from Harry with his cute and casual headband.

Harry has no problem pulling off this classic cut.

This tousled side-swept crop perfectly shows off Harry's natural waves.

A slicked back and sensible look for Harry's role in *My Policeman*.

Bed head but make it fashion.

QUIZ NAME YOUR DEBUT ALBUM

FIND YOUR ALBUM NAME USING THE GENERATOR BELOW. ALL YOU'LL NEED IS YOUR BIRTH MONTH AND YOUR FIRST INITIAL! PUT THE TWO WORDS TOGETHER AND HEY PRESTO... IT'S THAT EASY.

FIND YOUR BIRTH MONTH:

JANUARY	Haze
FEBRUARY	Joy
MARCH	Mirror
APRIL	Open
MAY	Brave
JUNE	Cloud
JULY	Hidden
AUGUST	Soul
SEPTEMBER	Mango
OCTOBER	Pop
NOVEMBER	Energy
DECEMBER	Clear

FIND YOUR FIRST INITIAL:

A	Magic
B	Dazzle
C	Wonder
D	Sugar
E	Indigo
F	Spark
G	Sweet
H	Feathers
I	Attention
J	Revival
K	High
L	Memories
M	Unforgotten

N	Kindness
O	Pure
P	Eccentric
Q	Turtle
R	Noon
S	Tattoo
T	Smile
U	Dusk
V	Style
W	Glam
X	Midnight
Y	Rainbow
Z	Times

Can you unscramble the letters to figure out the names of these three Harry Styles songs?

RAMTEWELGORNSUA

HOIGNFTESTIEMS

ASATWIS

" IF ONE HEART FITS ANOTHER LIKE A PUZZLE PIECE, MAYBE YOU COULD BE THE MISSING HALF OF ME... "

HARRY STYLES,
I'LL BE READY

9 SIGNS YOU'RE A HARRY SUPERFAN

HOW MANY OF THESE SOUND LIKE YOU? FIND OUT HOW MUCH OF A HARRY OBSESSIVE YOU REALLY ARE.

1 Whenever you're humming a tune, it's ALWAYS one of Harry's, and you don't even realize you're doing it. ☐

2 You're always the first of your friends to watch his music video releases. It's you who messages the group to let everyone know when it's dropped. ☐

3 You've read and watched every single one of his interviews out there... more than once! ☐

4 If you're faced with a tricky situation, you think to yourself, "What would Harry Styles do?" before making a decision. ☐

5 Your go-to daydream involves you meeting Harry. You're always practicing what you'll say to Harry if you meet him. ☐

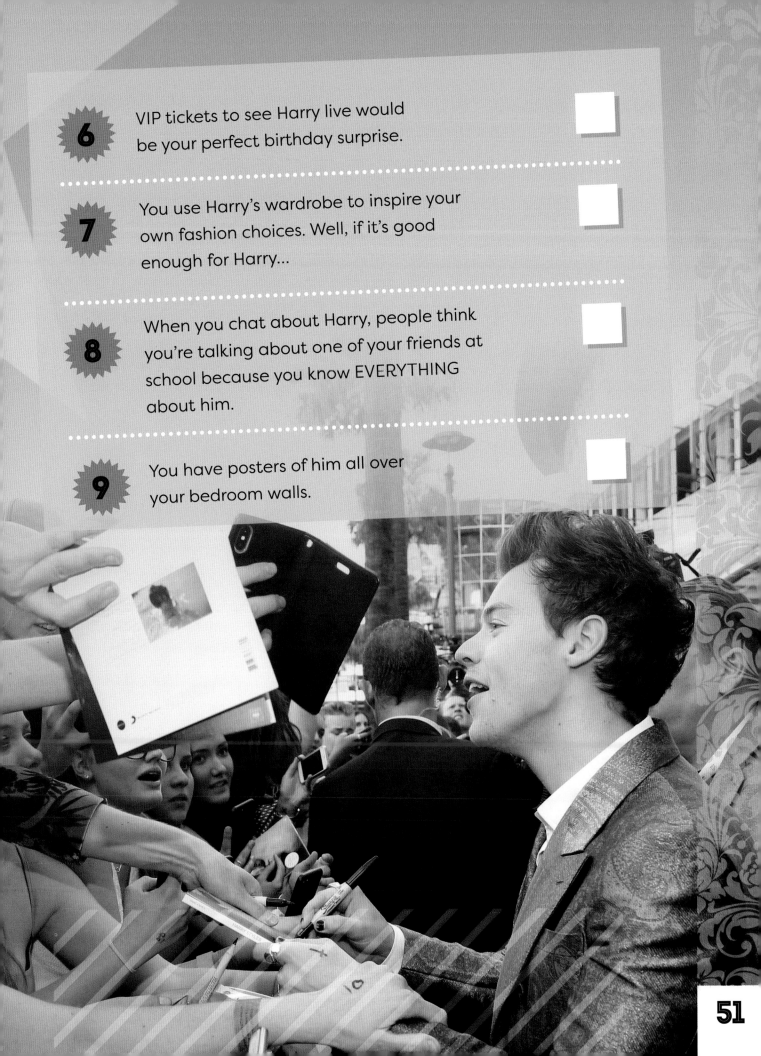

6 VIP tickets to see Harry live would be your perfect birthday surprise.

7 You use Harry's wardrobe to inspire your own fashion choices. Well, if it's good enough for Harry...

8 When you chat about Harry, people think you're talking about one of your friends at school because you know EVERYTHING about him.

9 You have posters of him all over your bedroom walls.

" I THINK WHEN YOU'RE WRITING SONGS, IT'S IMPOSSIBLE TO NOT DRAW ON PERSONAL EXPERIENCES, WHETHER IT BE TRAVELING OR GIRLS OR ANYTHING. "

HARRY STYLES

★ SPEAK UP!

STARS LIKE HARRY HAVE THE RARE OPPORTUNITY TO SHINE THE LIGHT ON IMPORTANT ISSUES AND INFLUENCE HUGE NUMBERS OF PEOPLE. HERE ARE A FEW OF THE WAYS THAT HARRY USES HIS PLATFORM POSITIVELY.

BLACK LIVES MATTER

Like many people during the Black Lives Matter protests in 2020, Harry was inspired to be more proactive. Besides taking part in marches, Harry spoke in interviews about the importance of being anti-racist. He admitted he hadn't been outspoken enough, but he wanted to change that. Harry also posted this on social media.

> " I DO THINGS EVERY DAY WITHOUT FEAR, BECAUSE I AM PRIVILEGED, AND I AM PRIVILEGED EVERY DAY BECAUSE I AM WHITE... BEING NOT RACIST IS NOT ENOUGH, WE MUST BE ANTI-RACIST. "
>
> **HARRY STYLES**

TO CELEBRATE PRIDE MONTH, HARRY SOLD SPECIAL RAINBOW-THEMED TREAT PEOPLE WITH KINDNESS T-SHIRTS. THE PROCEEDS WENT TO GLSEN, AN ORGANISATION THAT WORKS TO CREATE LGBTQ INCLUSIVE SCHOOLS.

LGBTQ+ ALLY

One of the things everyone loves about Harry is the positive environment he creates at his live performances. It's a safe space for everyone. He does this in so many ways, like by waving pride flags and telling the audience that no matter who they are or how they identify, he loves them. At one concert, Harry helped a fan to come out after she held up the sign that said, "I'm gonna come out to my parents because of you". Harry spotted the sign and got the whole crowd to support her.

REJECTS STEREOTYPES

Harry smashes the gender expectations that society puts on him. From painting his nails to wearing a dress on the cover of Vogue, Harry isn't about conforming. While he's certainly not the first male public figure to do this, he's definitely one of the most famous! Let's hope he's giving people the confidence to be themselves. Here he is with Alessandro Michele at the 2019 Met Gala (right).

SONG WRITING TIPS

COULD YOU BE THE NEXT CHART-TOPPING ARTIST? WELL, HERE ARE SOME TIPS AND TRICKS FOR HOW TO GO ABOUT IT. WHAT ARE YOU WAITING FOR?

BE AUTHENTIC!

Don't worry about what other people are doing, and never try to sound like anyone else.

WRITE FROM THE HEART

The best way to create something unique and personal is by writing about what you know.

WRITE EVERY DAY

Dedicate a time every day to sitting down and writing. Close your bedroom door and avoid any distractions, like TV or phones. It doesn't matter what you're writing, just get scribbling. Keeping a diary is a good place to start.

LISTEN TO MUSIC

The more the better! Listening to a variety of genres is a great way to discover what you love and can also be a brilliant source of inspiration.

GO OUTSIDE

Fresh air and just getting outside is almost always a good idea! You might be inspired to write about what you see, hear, or feel on your outing.

EMBRACE YOUR UNIQUENESS

Do you play a musical instrument, or can you rap? Inject as much personality as possible into your song. A track that doesn't sound like anybody else will make you memorable and also help you stand out.

HAVE FUN

Don't get caught up in trying to write something polished or perfect. Just go with the flow and write whatever comes to mind. You'll have plenty of time to tinker with it later down the line! The main thing is to get some words on the paper.

COLLABORATE!

If you're lacking that all important inspo, why not ask a friend to write a song with you? It might just be double the ideas and double the fun!

PLAY A GAME

Feeling stuck? Turn it into a game. Write down as many words as you can in one minute and see what you come up with. Then all you have to do is start stringing them together.

CHOOSE A THEME

Struggling to focus? Choosing a theme can help give you direction. How about love, family, friendship, vacations, or animals? Write about something you care about and know really well.

★ FAN GUIDE

IF YOU WANT TO KNOW HOW TO BECOME THE ULTIMATE STYLER, THEN THIS IS FOR YOU! FOLLOW THESE 9 STEPS, AND YOU'LL BE A HARRY STYLES SUPERFAN IN NO TIME.

1 Share your love of Harry with your friends to spread the joy. They may not realize quite how awesome he is yet!

2 Find other people who share your love of Harry—you could even build your own fan community.

3 Listen to all his albums. And if a pal is asking for music recommendations, always point them in the direction of one of Hazza's hits!

4 Embrace your individuality just like Harry, and wear what makes you feel happy— even if it's not what your friends are into.

5 Read or watch as many of his interviews as you can get your mitts on. Harry is so witty and so wise!

6 Check out Harry's musical influences. From reading this book you now know he loves Elvis, Shania Twain, and many more. Head to page 20 for more ideas.

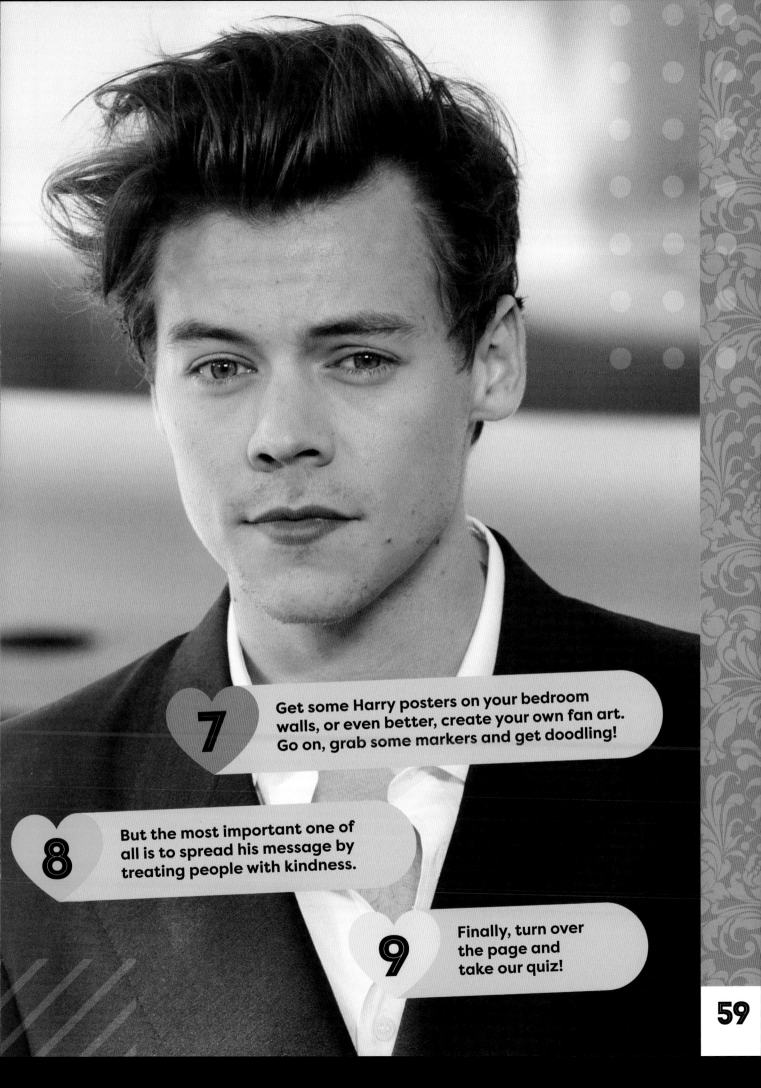

7 Get some Harry posters on your bedroom walls, or even better, create your own fan art. Go on, grab some markers and get doodling!

8 But the most important one of all is to spread his message by treating people with kindness.

9 Finally, turn over the page and take our quiz!

HOW WELL DO YOU KNOW HARRY?

PUT YOUR KNOWLEDGE TO THE TEST WITH THIS MEGA-FUN HARRY QUIZ.

1 What was the name of Harry's first solo single?

2 Who features in the *Treat People with Kindness* music video with Harry?

3 Name the first movie Harry was in.

4 What is the name of Harry's sister?

5 If Harry wasn't a singer, what would he be?

A. Teacher
B. Builder
C. Lawyer
D. Dancer

6 Where was Harry's Saturday job as a teenager?

7 Which of these is NOT a Harry Styles song?

A. *Grapejuice*
B. *Satellite*
C. *Little Freak*
D. *Late Night Walking*

8 Apart from English, which other language can Harry speak?

A. Welsh
B. French
C. Spanish
D. German

9 What is Harry's favorite animal?

10 What's the name of Harry's beauty brand?

11 What was the name of Harry's band at school?

12 Who was the youngest member of 1D?

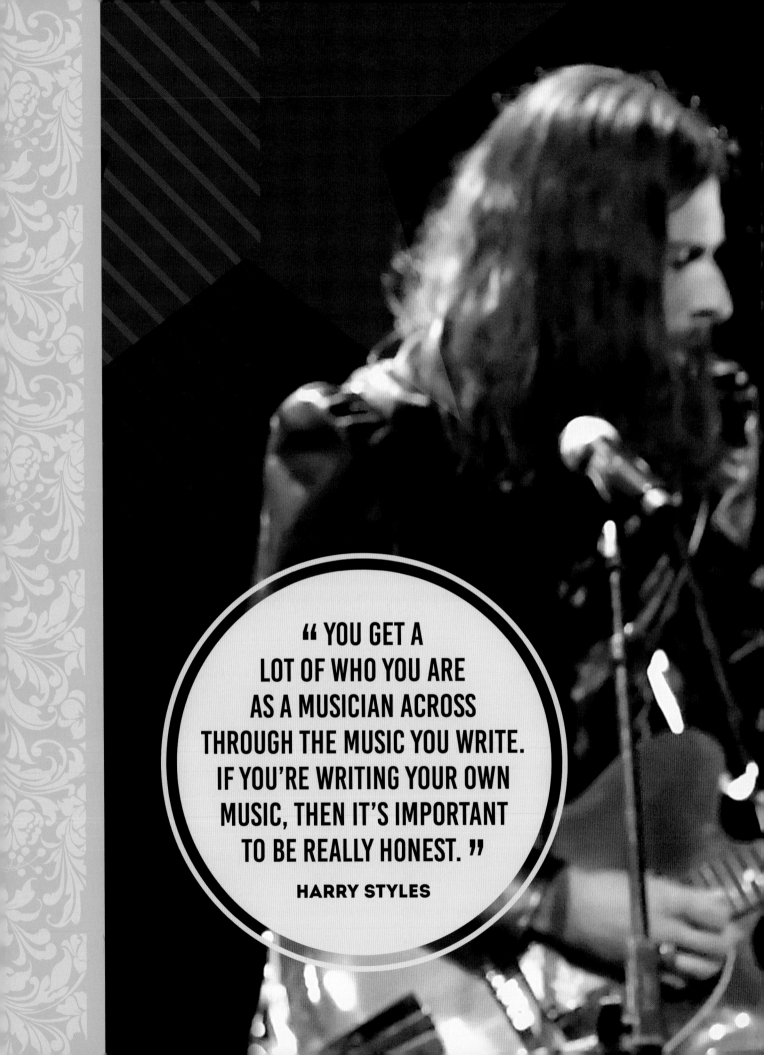

" YOU GET A LOT OF WHO YOU ARE AS A MUSICIAN ACROSS THROUGH THE MUSIC YOU WRITE. IF YOU'RE WRITING YOUR OWN MUSIC, THEN IT'S IMPORTANT TO BE REALLY HONEST. "

HARRY STYLES

TREAT PEOPLE WITH KINDNESS!

························ · · · · · ··········

TPWK